FU
JOB

A journal for employees
to destroy, rant and vent
without losing their jobs

By Alex A. Lluch

WS Publishing Group
San Diego, California 92119

FU JOB
A journal for employees to destroy,
rant and vent without losing their jobs

By Alex A. Lluch
Published by WS Publishing Group
San Diego, California 92119
© Copyright 2010 by WS Publishing Group

Design by:
David Defenbaugh, Sarah Jang; WS Publishing Group

Image credits:
bonsai tree © iStockphoto/adroach
party people icon © iStockphoto

For more information on this and many other best-selling books visit
www.WSPublishingGroup.com.
E-mail: info@WSPublishingGroup.com

ISBN 13: 978-1-934386-95-8
Printed in China

Reply All:

Draft the email you would
like to send to everyone at your job.

Send

aka
abbreviation

1: also known as
<My boss: aka "Blowhard">

anonym • moniker • alias • nom de plume • pseudonym

aka
BOSS

Make a list of the nicknames you
give your boss behind his or her back.

rather
adverb

1: more readily or willingly
<I would rather be eating paint
chips than doing this lame job>

considerably • noticeably • quite • much • very

I'd RATHER be...

Make a list of things you'd rather be doing than working. Such as plucking your eyelashes out one by one.

bulls•eye
noun

3: something that precisely attains a desired end
<It's easy to get a bullseye when my boss' face
is the target>

direct hit • center • target • homerun • hole in one

Bullseye

Label this voodoo doll as your boss or most hated coworker. Tear it out, hang it on the wall, and throw darts at it.

HELLO
my name is

stream of con•scious•ness
noun

1: the continuous unedited
chronological flow of conscious
experience through the mind
<No one wants to be in my
stream of consciousness>

free association • inner monologue • train of thought

FU Stream of Consciousness

Write down the first thoughts that come to your mind:

Meetings:

Email forwards:

Vacation time:

Cubicles:

Mondays:

Your boss:

Talkative coworkers:

Overtime:

Coffee:

Team-building exercises:

feng shui
noun

1: Chinese practice in which a site is configured so as to harmonize with the spiritual forces that inhabit it
<My dirty desk needs some serious feng shui>

redesign • makeover • redecoration • reorganize

office
FENG SHUI

This is your chance to redecorate your cubicle.

Paste cutouts or draw on this page.

crush
verb

1 a: to squeeze or force by pressure
so as to destroy
b: to reduce to particles by
pounding or grinding
<I will crush my boss' car if he
doesn't give me a raise>

smash • break • destroy • bruise • pulverize • squeeze

Which office appliance would you like to

crush

in a giant vise?

< Error! >

< Invalid entry >

< Shutting down >

LIST THINGS TO CRUSH HERE

quit
verb

1 a: to depart from or out of
b: to leave the company of
<I will quit this job by yelling "FU, suckers!">

give up • step down • drop • abandon • vacate

I QUIT!

Yell "I quit!" as loud as you can into these pages. *

* Don't do this at work.

waste
verb

1: to spend or use carelessly
<You waste my time with
these stupid meetings>

squander • dissipate • fritter • use up • misspend

WASTE precious work time.

Tear out this page and make it into **origami.**

perk
noun

1: a privilege, gain, or profit
incidental to regular salary or wage
<One perk of this job is that I can
sleep under my desk>

bonus • advantage • prize • extra • fringe benefit

Work
PERK

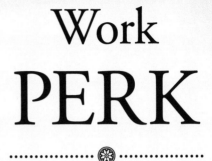

·················· ❁ ··················

Come up with a few things you
DON'T hate about your job.
Like free black tar coffee.
Write your list here.

drunkard
noun

1: one who is habitually drunk
<Being the office drunkard is a
real honor>

boozer • carouser • barfly • sloppy mess • wino

kiss ass
noun

1: someone who acts obsequiously
especially to gain favor
<She is such a kiss ass I want to scream>

brownnoser • suck up • flatterer • lackey • pet

FU kiss ass

Who is the biggest kiss ass at your job?

_____

_____

_____

_____

_____

_____

_____

_____

_____

TELL HIM OR HER OFF HERE

nev•er
adverb

1: not ever; at no time
<I am never going to return from vacation>

by no means • rarely • in no way • not under any condition

Be back NEVER.

Write the Out of Office Reply you wish you could post.

SEND NOW   SEND LATER   DELETE   PRIORITY

Out of Office Message:

....
....
....
....
....
....
....
....
....
....
....
....

de•face
verb

1 a: to corrupt the purity or perfection of
<I will feel better after I deface
this journal>

abuse • besmirch • dirty • pollute • sully • tarnish

DEFACE

this page with as many office
supplies as you can.

blunt
adjective

3 a: abrupt in speech or manner
b: being straight to the point
<Let me be blunt: You suck>

direct • unsubtle • outspoken • honest • candid

Dear ....,

Let me be BLUNT.

You are most the miserable ....

.... I have ever had.

Working with you makes me want to ....

....

When you talk to me about ....

....,

I want to scream. I won't tell you to your face,

but you ....

....

I wish I could throw ....

at you. Why don't you move to ....

.... for .... years?

Sincerely,

Ouch!

....

lei•sure
noun

1: freedom provided by the cessation of activities;
time free from work or duties
<Work interferes with my leisure time>

pleasure • ease • freedom • holiday • own sweet time

brain•storm
verb

1: to solve a problem or create an idea by
thinking intensely on it
<Let's brainstorm new ways to waste work time>

share • invent • dream up • put our heads together

FU

Brainstorm

Write down as many four-letter
words as you can think of
in 1 minute.

f # @ k

gos•sip
noun

1 a: a person who habitually reveals personal or
sensational facts about others
b: an officious or inquisitive person
<I am constantly spied on by the office gossip>

busybody • buttinsky • eavesdropper • rubbernecker

scrib•ble
verb

1: to write hastily or carelessly without regard to
legibility or form
2: to cover with careless writings or drawings
<I am going to scribble on this page until I stop
wanting to punch my boss>

draw • scrawl • doodle • scratch • grind • grate • sketch

GET A RED PEN.
SCRIBBLE
on this page as **hard** as you can.

cel•e•brate
verb

2 a: to honor by refraining from ordinary business
b: to mark by festivities or other deviation from
routine
<I will celebrate if I get fired>

party • paint the town red • let loose • rejoice • fiesta

CELEBRATE
the end of your
workday.

TEAR
this page into tiny
pieces of confetti
and throw them
up in the air.

sucking
verb

1: to draw something in by or as if
by exerting a suction force
<Monday morning meetings are
sucking my will to live>

drain • empty • fatigue • exhaust • dishearten

This job is
sucking
the life out of me.

Write down the number of years this
job has probably taken off your life.

work•place
noun

1: a place where work is done
<Workplace Word Search is a great
way to distract myself from doing
actual work>

shop • factory • office • store • site • plant

Workplace Word Search

```
i w c l k f c e v p r i n t e r
e t a b u s y c a s e c n d r d
o u t r b n e y c r m w r w d d
e t u m m o c d a s w a e a m i
o o c c y h s h t c o t l r z i
a y i e e r o s i v r e p u s y
i s c c e d a b o j k r a f p a
y i k o h y o t n t p c t i e d
a a i f k r o c e s l o s r n n
d a d f c e e l s r a o e e c o
i n s i o k o e p s c l k d i m
r s k c l r n m z m e e a e l p
f n p e c o m p u t e r s r r e
o e a v h w h t o w i m d i y a
s m i p g o s s i p u u o h s n
f i r e d c u b i c l e q n p b
```

Fired	Job	Monday	Employee
Secretary	Vacation	Workplace	Pencil
Hired	Commute	Crazy	Phone
Boss	Lunch	Nap	Printer
Holiday	Watercooler	Cubicle	Friday
Stapler	Computer	Office	Quit
Busy	Memo	Desk	Gossip
Supervisor	Weekend	Dresscode	Salary
Clock	Coworker	Paycheck	

re•sig•na•tion
noun

1: the act of giving oneself over without resistance
<I had no choice but turn in my resignation from
this hellhole>

fold • quit • throw in the towel • retire • step down

Draft your letter of
RESIGNATION

Dear ....,

....

....

....

....

....

....

....

....

....

....

....

Sincerely,

....

P.S. This job sucks. I'm outta here.

Addendum: Don't turn this in; unless you really want to quit, that is.

va•moose
verb

1: to depart quickly, to disappear
<I am packed and ready to
vamoose>

run away • bolt • escape • quit • make a break for it

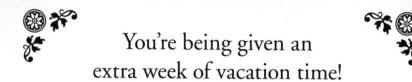

You're being given an
extra week of vacation time!

Where do you
VAMOOSE TO?

Paste a picture here

Poof!

team building
noun

1: exercises for improving motivation, communication, support and trust within a team
<I consider office happy hour valid team building>

collaboration • cooperation • synergy • working together

FU Team Building

Tear out this page and fold it into a paper football.

Find a coworker who is just **as miserable as you** and play at his or her desk.

TD!

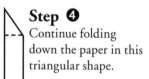

Step ❹
Continue folding down the paper in this triangular shape.

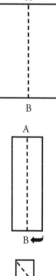

Step ❶
Take a regular 8.5 x 11 sheet of paper, and cut or fold it in half along line AB.

Step ❺
When you have folded your paper to a point, tuck the rectangular remainder at the end of the triangle into the pocket created by the folds of your paper. Now go waste some valuable work time!

Step ❷
Fold the remaining half of the paper in half along line AB.

Step ❸
Now fold along this line to create a triangular fold. The dotted line should be the top of your paper.

busi•ness
noun

3: dealings or transactions especially of
an economic nature
<I like to do business in flip-flops>

administration • tactic • procedure • protocol • red tape

BUSINESS CASUAL

 Paste magazine cutouts of what you
wish you could wear to work here.

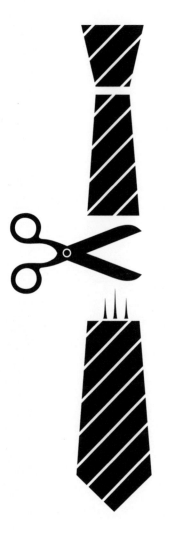

OFFICE DRESS CODE BE DAMNED!

memo
noun

1: an informal record written
reminder
<I sent a memo to my coworkers
to waste their time>

letter • announcement • directive • message • missive

Memo:
Waste some time.
Draw a picture on
this page.

des•cribe
verb

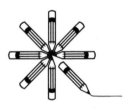

1: to represent or give an account of in
words
<There are no words to describe how
much I hate my job>

delineate • depict • draw • portray • illustrate • outline

Describe your
job...as you know it.

....

....

....

....

....

....

....

....

....

....

....

....

paint
verb

1: to treat with a liquid by
brushing or swabbing
<I like to paint with White Out
because it gives me a buzz>

decorate • adorn • touch up • apply • color • cover

PAINT

this entire page with a
bottle of White Out.

(Don't sniff it.)

hell
noun

2: a place or state of misery, torment, or wickedness
<I am beginning to think this office is hell>

horror • torment • anguish • bad dream • underworld

dec•o•rate
verb

2: to furnish with something ornamental
<I like to decorate my report
with coffee stains>

adorn • beautify • dress • embellish • bedeck • garnish

DECORATE

this page

using your crappy office coffee
like it is watercolor paint.

this coffee
is blah

ran•som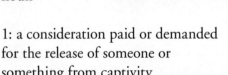
noun

1: a consideration paid or demanded
for the release of someone or
something from captivity
<I am holding my boss' stapler for
ransom until she gives me a raise>

captive • pawn • prisoner • payoff • bribe • hostage

FU Ransom

Cut out letters to make a ransom-style note and leave it for your coworkers to see.

IF YOU EVER WAnt to SeE YOUR StapleR...

A a a a A B b b C c c D d

d E E e E e F F f G g g H

h h I i i I i J j j K K k L l

l M m m M N n n O o o O

o P p P Q q q R r r S s S

s t t T T u U U u U V v v

W w w X x x Y y y Z z z

1 2 3 4 5 6 7 8 9 0 = + "

" ! @ # $ % ^ & * ? ( ) , .

strand•ed
verb

1: to leave in a strange or
unfavorable place especially
without funds or means to depart
<I would hate to be stranded with
this creep>

stuck • beached • disabled • marooned • wrecked

You are STRANDED

on a desert island with your boss.

What are three things you wish you had?

❸

stomp
verb

1: to tread heavily so as to
bruise, crush, or injure
<I would like to stomp on my
boss' face>

 trample • smash • squash • pound • crush • scuff

STOMP

on this page with
your dirty shoe.

road rage
noun

1: a motorist's uncontrolled anger or
violence that is usually provoked by
another motorist's irritating act
<I get road rage every single morning>

anger • fury • violent outburst • explosion

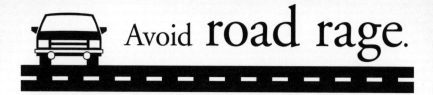

Avoid road rage.

Vent about your commute to work here.

mon•day
noun

1: the first day of the workweek
<Don't talk to me on Monday
before I have caffeine>

pale • exhausted • wan • beat • haggard • grumpy

Draw a picture of yourself on

MONDAY MORNING

without coffee.

ME +  =

team•work
verb

1: work done by several associates
with each doing a part
<I'm going to kick this journal at the
next person who says, "There is no 'I' in teamwork">

collaboration • cooperation • partnership • togetherness

TEAMWORK

PUNT this book across the room to a coworker.

Have him or her punt it back to you.

shut up
verb

1: to cause a person to stop talking
<I wish I could tell my boss to shut up>

clam up • hush • quiet down • zip it • settle • refrain

shut UP!

 Point this page at someone in your workplace.
Enjoy the blissful silence.

hap•py
adjective

3 a : enjoying or characterized by
well-being and contentment
<When I imagine not being at work, I feel happy>

delighted • blissful • peaceful • joyful • pleased

Go to your

 **H**appy place.

Paste cutouts from
magazines here to make a
collage of a spot that makes
you feel serene.

My Happy Place

hand•book

noun

1: a book conveniently covering
one subject
<Our employee handbook was
written by a bunch of morons>

guide • manual • primer • reference • instructions

FU Office Handbook

What is one office policy you would like to implement?

Dear Coworkers,

Please note that the following policy will be effective immediately:

All individuals who object to this policy can suck it!

as•sess•ment
noun

1: the action of appraisal
<My assessment of this job is, it stinks and I hate it>

evaluation • appraisal • value • computation

FU Career
ASSESSMENT FORM

❈ ❈ ❈ Would you rather? ❈ ❈ ❈

❑ Make a little money at a job you love ••• OR ••• ❑ Make a lot of money at a job you hate?

❑ Walk Pitbulls for a living ••• OR ••• ❑ Make drinks at Starbucks?

❑ Get a promotion ••• OR ••• ❑ Get a new job?

❑ Eat a live bug ••• OR ••• ❑ Spend the weekend with your boss?

❑ Have a 4-day workweek ••• OR ••• ❑ Win $10,000?

❑ Work from home ••• OR ••• ❑ Own your own business?

❑ Work at this job for the next 30 years ••• OR ••• ❑ Lose your possessions in a fire?

❑ Get a company car ••• OR ••• ❑ Get your own office?

Submit to management upon completion   For office use only ❑❑❑❑

crap•py
adjective

1: markedly inferior in quality, lousy
<All parts of my job are crappy in
their own way>

crummy • junky • lousy • shoddy • inferior • third rate

CRAPPY FACTOR
Graph Analysis

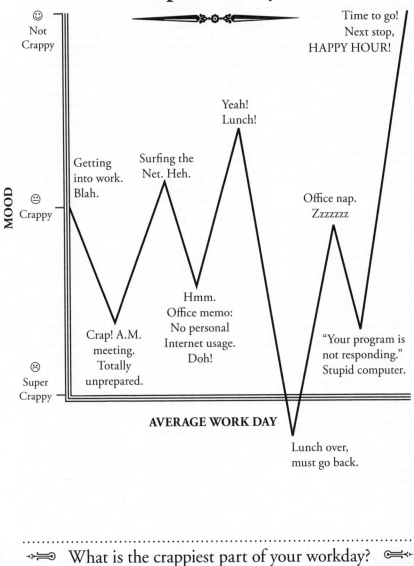

....
→➤ What is the crappiest part of your workday? ➤←

resumé
noun

1: a short statement of the main points
<My resumé exemplifies all of the
reasons why I am overqualified and
underpaid>

summary • encapsulation • outline • vitae • synopsis

MY RESUMÉ

Naturally, you're totally unappreciated.

Give your resumé a facelift and resubmit it for a promotion.

❀ **Career Objective:**
(i.e. To work as little as possible)

❀ **Previous Work Experience:**
(i.e. I am not at liberty to discuss)

❀ **Skills:**
(i.e. Can touch my nose with my tongue)

❀ **Education & Training:**
(i.e. Attended the school of hard knocks)

❀ **Additional Qualifications:**
(i.e. Top score on Grand Theft Auto)

nem•e•sis
noun

2: a formidable and usually
victorious rival or opponent
<My boss is my nemesis because
he takes credit for my work>

rival • enemy • punisher • scourge • vigilante

NEMESIS

Have you ever been backstabbed
by a coworker? Vent about it.

....
....
....
....
....
....
....
....
....
....
....
....
....

ro•mance
noun

1: a romantic attachment or episode between lovers
<My boss put the kibosh on office romance ever since
that incident in the supply closet>

affair • amour • flirtation • infatuation • fling • liaison

Office Romance

Name one coworker
you'd make out with.

Now FOLD up the corners of this page and
STAPLE them shut. Take this to your grave.

rules
noun

1: a prescribed guide for conduct or action
<I like to break the rules by surfing the Internet
all day long>

bylaw • regulation • code • law • ordinance • command

RULES are meant to be broken.

What are your favorite office rules to BREAK?

par•ty
noun

3: a social gathering
<I dance on my desk every time we have an
office party >

affair • blowout • fete • function • shindig • gala

Office PARTY!

Imagine you win the
Lottery jackpot.
What would you do?

....

....

....

....

....

....

spell
noun

1 a: spoken word or form of words
held to have magic power
<I am working on a spell that will turn
my boss into a pig>

bewitchment • charm • enchantment • incantation

Cast a SPELL

on someone at work who annoys the CRAP out of you!

INSTRUCTIONS:

- Pour ½ cup of red wine into a bowl.

- Take a pen from your office.
  Break it and pour the ink into the mixture.

- Add two dashes of salt.

- Drop in a pinch of staples.

- Mix counterclockwise.

Now, check off which misfortune you want the spell to give your foe.

☐ Overtime without pay

☐ All computer files suddenly disappear

☐ Can't find his or her car keys

☐ Grow a tail

☐ Can't speak for a week

quote
noun

1: a sentence or phrase used to motivate and inspire
<I chant this quote to stay calm when I want to scream>

slogan • motto • byword • epigram • maxim • proverb

Write down a

MOTIVATIONAL

QUOTE

"

Yes, this can help.

MAYBE

hush-hush
adjective

1: marked by, held in, or conducted with secrecy
<We all knew about the CEO's hush-hush
relationship with the cleaning lady>

illicit • on the sly • clandestine • undercover • covert

HUSH-HUSH

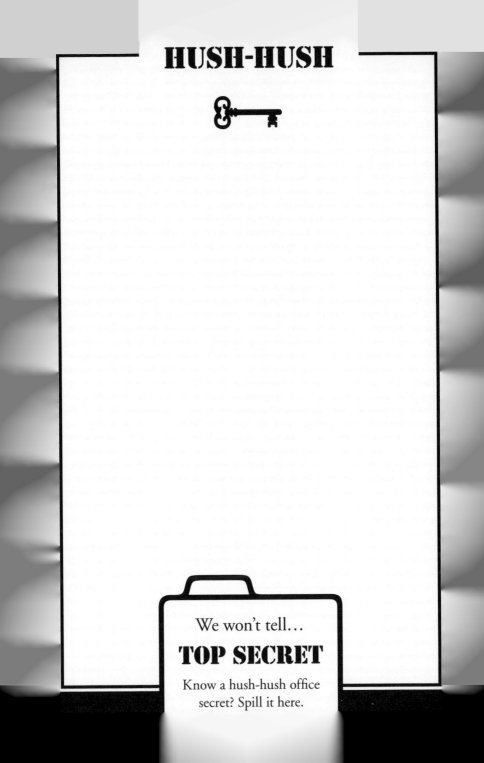

We won't tell…

TOP SECRET

Know a hush-hush office
secret? Spill it here.

award
noun

2: something that is conferred or
bestowed especially on the basis of merit
<I present you with the award for the
shadiest coworker>

distinction • honor • prize • badge • accolade • ribbon

FU Employee AWARDS

NAME YOUR _____ COWORKER

 Laziest:

 Loudest:

 Friendliest:

 Smartest:

 Most incompetent:

 Most dramatic:

 Most boring:

 Most impatient:

 Most creative:

 Shadiest:

con•grat•u•la•tions
noun

1: complementing someone on an
achievement or success
<Congratulations: You are the biggest
idiot in this office>

hooray • compliments • felicitations • applause

Congratulations!

_____

Name

Is awarded this

CERTIFICATE OF ACHIEVEMENT

for distinction as the worst person
to work with on the planet.

Presented this _____ day of _____ in the year _____

Signed by _____

bom•bard
verb

2: to assail vigorously or
persistently
<I can waste time by
bombarding my unsuspecting
officemates with spitballs>

assail • batter • fire upon • pester • barrage • pelt

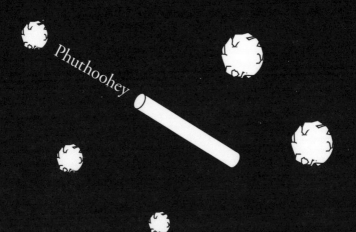

Phuthoohey

BOMBARD

a coworker with spitballs you
make out of this page.

Phuthoohey

buzz•word
noun

1: an important-sounding usually technical word or
phrase often of little meaning used chiefly
to impress laymen
<I can't make sense of my boss's buzzwords>

bunk • cliché • mumbo jumbo • lingo • nonsense

BUZZWORD

Keep me in the loop	PROACTIVE	Dynamic	Dropped the ball	User-friendly
CC ME	Moving forward	Synergy	Streamline	Let's touch base
Deliverables	Prioritize	**FREE SPACE**	BRAIN-STORMING SESSION	Think outside the box
Disseminate	Onboard	Strategic	Word-of-mouth	ASSETS
EMPOWER	Run with it	What's on your plate?	Just following up	Win-Win

BiNGO

Place a paperclip in the square each time you hear this annoying workplace jargon.

ex•cuse
noun

1: to try to remove blame from
<My dog makes a crappy excuse for missing meetings>

alibi • cover story • explanation • whitewash • justification

What is your favorite EXCUSE for being late to work?

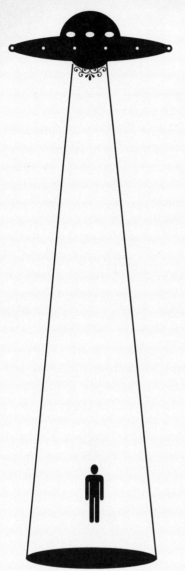

"Uh, would you believe
I was abducted by aliens?
Seriously, no really."

re•cy•cle
verb

1: to make a substance available for reuse for
biological activities
<My filing system consists of placing important
documents in the recycle bin>

toss out • revamp • reuse • reinvent • scrap

place junk here

FU RECYCLE

Make an effort to be green. Tape random objects, sticky notes and other pieces of junk from your desk to this page to make a collage.
Call it art and write it off as work time.

ig•nore
verb

1: to refuse to take notice of
<My officemate's voice is so loud that it is
impossible to ignore>

neglect • disregard • overlook • shrug off • shirk

Fend off talkative coworkers.
Cut out this message and hang it in your workspace.

※

fin•ger
noun

1: any of the five terminating members
of the hand
<I give my boss the finger every time
he walks away>

※

index • middle • ring • thumb • pinkie

the fnger

day•dream
verb

1: to have a pleasant visionary or wishful
creation of the imagination
<I like to daydream that I work at Disneyland>

muse • imagine • fantasize • pipe dream • stargaze

You can still

DAYDREAM ...

Name all the jobs you'd rather
have than your own.

1

2

3

pissed
adjective

1: bitter in spirit: irritated
<Caution: pissed off driver behind the wheel>

bitter • dismal • crestfallen • annoyed • dejected

Pissed off and driving to work? Create a FU Bumper Sticker to warn other people on the road.

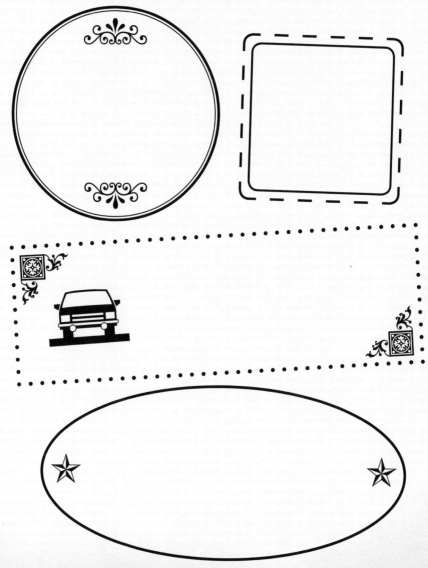

loos•en up
verb

1: to become less tense
<I need to loosen up with a stiff
drink>

balm • pacify • placate • calm • tranquilize • ease

LOOSEN THE

f#@k up

Make a list of the ways
you can de-stress (or sedate
yourself) after work.

dream
noun

1: a strongly desired goal or purpose
<My dream is to quit this miserable job and
get a cooler one>

vision • fantasy • aim • ambition • aspiration